THE QUEEN'S BROADCAST

FRIDAY SEPTEMBER 5

'I WANT TO PAY TRIBUTE TO DIANA MYSELF. SHE WAS AN EXCEPTIONAL AND GIFTED HUMAN BEING. IN GOOD TIMES AND BAD, SHE NEVER LOST HER CAPACITY TO SMILE AND LAUGH, NOR TO INSPIRE OTHERS WITH HER WARMTH AND KINDNESS. I ADMIRED AND RESPECTED HER – FOR HER ENERGY AND COMMITMENT TO OTHERS, AND ESPECIALLY FOR HER DEVOTION TO HER TWO BOYS. NO ONE WHO KNEW DIANA WILL EVER FORGET HER. MILLIONS OF OTHERS WHO NEVER MET HER, BUT FELT THEY KNEW HER, WILL REMEMBER HER. THIS IS ALSO AN OPPORTUNITY FOR ME, ON BEHALF OF MY FAMILY, AND ESPECIALLY PRINCE CHARLES AND WILLIAM AND HARRY, TO THANK ALL OF YOU WHO HAVE BROUGHT FLOWERS, SENT MESSAGES AND PAID YOUR RESPECTS IN SO MANY WAYS TO A REMARKABLE PERSON. THESE ACTS OF KINDNESS HAVE BEEN A HUGE SOURCE OF HELP AND COMFORT. OUR THOUGHTS ARE ALSO WITH DIANA'S FAMILY AND THE FAMILIES OF THOSE WHO DIED WITH HER. I KNOW THAT THEY TOO HAVE DRAWN STRENGTH FROM WHAT HAS HAPPENED SINCE LAST WEEKEND, AS THEY SEEK TO HEAL THEIR SORROW AND THEN TO FACE THE FUTURE WITHOUT A LOVED ONE. MAY THOSE WHO DIED REST IN PEACE AND MAY WE, EACH AND EVERY ONE OF US, THANK GOD FOR SOMEONE WHO MADE MANY, MANY PEOPLE HAPPY.'

EARL SPENCER'S TRIBUTE

SATURDAY SEPTEMBER 6

'DIANA WAS A SYMBOL OF SELFLESS HUMANITY ALL OVER THE WORLD. A STANDARD BEARER FOR THE RIGHTS OF THE TRULY DOWNTRODDEN, A VERY BRITISH GIRL WHO TRANSCENDED NATIONALITY. SOMEONE WHO WAS CLASSLESS AND WHO PROVED IN THE LAST YEAR THAT SHE NEEDED NO ROYAL TITLE TO CONTINUE TO GENERATE HER PARTICULAR BRAND OF MAGIC. WE WILL ALL FEEL CHEATED ALWAYS THAT YOU WERE TAKEN FROM US SO YOUNG AND YET WE MUST LEARN TO BE GRATEFUL THAT YOU CAME ALONG AT ALL. ONLY NOW THAT YOU ARE GONE DO WE TRULY APPRECIATE WHAT WE ARE NOW WITHOUT, AND WE WANT YOU TO KNOW THAT LIFE WITHOUT YOU IS VERY, VERY DIFFICULT. YOUR JOY FOR LIFE TRANSMITTED WHERE EVER YOU TOOK YOUR SMILE AND THE SPARKLE IN THOSE UNFORGETTABLE EYES. YOUR BOUNDLESS ENERGY WHICH YOU COULD BARELY CONTAIN. WITHOUT YOUR GOD-GIVEN SENSITIVITY WE WOULD BE IMMERSED IN GREATER IGNORANCE AT THE ANGUISH OF AIDS AND HIV SUFFERERS, THE PLIGHT OF THE HOMELESS, THE ISOLATION OF LEPERS, THE RANDOM DESTRUCTION OF LAND MINES. SHE WOULD WANT US TODAY TO PLEDGE OURSELVES TO PROTECTING HER BELOVED BOYS WILLIAM AND HARRY. WE WILL NOT ALLOW THEM TO SUFFER THE ANGUISH THAT USED REGULARLY TO DRIVE YOU TO TEARFUL DESPAIR. AND BEYOND THAT, ON BEHALF OF YOUR MOTHER AND SISTERS, I PLEDGE THAT WE, YOUR BLOOD FAMILY, WILL DO ALL WE CAN TO CONTINUE THE IMAGINATIVE WAY IN WHICH YOU WERE STEERING THESE TWO EXCEPTIONAL YOUNG MEN SO THAT THEIR SOULS ARE NOT SIMPLY IMMERSED BY DUTY AND TRADITION BUT CAN SING OPENLY AS YOU PLANNED. WE FULLY RESPECT THE HERITAGE INTO WHICH THEY HAVE BOTH BEEN BORN AND WILL ALWAYS ENCOURAGE THEM IN THEIR ROYAL ROLE BUT WE, LIKE YOU, RECOGNISE THE NEED FOR THEM TO EXPERIENCE AS MANY DIFFERENT ASPECTS OF LIFE AS POSSIBLE TO ARM THEM SPIRITUALLY AND EMOTIONALLY FOR THE YEARS AHEAD. WILLIAM AND HARRY, WE ALL CARED DESPERATELY FOR YOU TODAY. WE ARE ALL CHEWED UP WITH THE SADNESS AT THE LOSS OF A WOMAN WHO WAS NOT EVEN YOUR MOTHER. HOW GREAT YOUR SUFFERING IS, WE CANNOT EVEN IMAGINE.'

The Funeral

THE YOUNG PRINCES HAD REMAINED AT BALMORAL
TO PREPARE FOR THEIR MOTHER'S FUNERAL. BUT
NOTHING COULD HAVE PREPARED THEM, OR THEIR
FATHER, FOR THE FORCE OF PUBLIC FEELING THAT
WOULD DEVELOP AFTER DIANA'S DEATH. ON THE EVE
OF THE FUNERAL, PRINCE CHARLES ACCOMPANIED
PRINCES WILLIAM AND HARRY TO KENSINGTON PALACE,
WHERE THEY WERE OVERWHELMED BY THE CROWDS
OF MOURNERS – JUST SOME OF THE HUNDREDS
OF THOUSANDS OF PEOPLE WHO KEPT VIGIL FOR
THE YOUNG PRINCES' BELOVED MOTHER.

FOUR PRINCES AND AN EARL SOLEMNLY TOOK THEIR
PLACES BEHIND THE GUN CARRIAGE WHICH CARRIED
DIANA, PRINCESS OF WALES, TO WESTMINSTER ABBEY.
THEIR MILE-LONG JOURNEY WAS LINED 15-PEOPLE DEEP
WITH MEMBERS OF THE PUBLIC WHO HAD TURNED
OUT IN EVEN GREATER NUMBERS THAN FOR THE ROYAL
WEDDING IN 1981. WHILE 2,000 MOURNERS WAITED IN
THE ABBEY, A CROWD OF 50,000 LINED THE CORTEGE
ROUTE ON KENSINGTON HIGH STREET ALONE, AND
30,000 PEOPLE CAMPED OUT IN LONDON THE NIGHT
BEFORE. TV BROUGHT THE FUNERAL TO 25 MILLION
VIEWERS IN THE UK AND 2.5 BILLION WORLDWIDE.

DRAPED WITH AN ERMINE-LINED ROYAL STANDARD,
DIANA'S COFFIN – WEIGHING 40 STONE – WAS CARRIED
THROUGH HYDE PARK, ALONG CONSTITUTION HILL AND
THE MALL BY THE KING'S TROOP GUN CARRIAGE. IT WAS
A STATE FUNERAL IN ALL BUT NAME. YET, IN KEEPING
WITH THE PRINCESS'S INFORMAL STYLE, THERE WERE
NO GUN SALUTES OR MILITARY MUSIC. THE CROWD WAS
HUSHED AND ON TOP OF THE STANDARD WERE THREE
WREATHS OF WHITE FLOWERS. ONE, OF SMALL ROSEBUDS,
CARRIED A SIMPLE WHITE ENVELOPE BEARING JUST
ONE WORD: 'MUMMY'. AS THE CORTEGE PASSED, MORE
FLOWERS WERE CAST BEFORE IT BY THE SILENT CROWD

The Royal Marriage

OVER 750 MILLION PEOPLE WORLDWIDE WATCHED
THE WEDDING OF THE CENTURY ON TELEVISION.
IT WAS PERHAPS THE GREATEST DISPLAY OF PAGEANTRY
THIS COUNTRY HAS EVER PRODUCED.
PRESIDENTS, KINGS AND CELEBRITIES FLOCKED TO
WITNESS THE FAIRYTALE WEDDING AT ST PAUL'S
CATHEDRAL. AND WITH A SINGLE KISS, DIANA CAPTURED
HER PRINCE – AND THE HEARTS OF A NATION.

DIANA WOULD LATER REVEAL HOW TERRIFIED SHE
WAS ON THE DAY SHE MARRIED. HER NERVES DIDN'T
SHOW AND SHE BASKED IN THE CHEERS FROM THE
CROWD THAT LINED THE ROUTE TO BUCKINGHAM
PALACE. THE WHOLE NATION CELEBRATED WITH
STREET PARTIES ACROSS THE LAND. FROM THIS DAY
FORWARD, SHE WOULD BECOME THE WORLD'S
MOST FAMOUS AND PHOTOGRAPHED WOMAN

DESPITE HER WORRIES – ABOUT THE BULIMIA
THAT HAD PLAGUED HER ENGAGEMENT, AND HER
HUSBAND'S FRIENDSHIP WITH CAMILLA PARKER

THE BIRTH OF PRINCE HENRY ON SEPTEMBER 15 1984
SEEMED TO MAKE THE FAMILY COMPLETE BUT, BEHIND
THE SMILES, DIANA'S WORLD WAS BEGINNING TO FALL
APART. SHE WAS DETERMINED, HOWEVER, TO MAKE
THE MARRIAGE WORK SO HER CHILDREN WOULD
NOT ENDURE THE PAIN SHE HAD FELT DURING HER
OWN PARENT'S DIVORCE. AND PRINCE CHARLES –
HIMSELF THE PRODUCT OF A RATHER FROSTY
UPBRINGING – WANTED TO GIVE THE BOYS THE
WARMTH AND AFFECTION HE HAD NOT BEEN
SHOWN. TO THE WATCHING WORLD, THEY
WERE A PERFECT FAMILY.

Her Family

AND FRIENDS

DIANA WAS DEVASTATED AS A CHILD WHEN HER PARENTS
DIVORCED IN 1969. A MONTH LATER HER MOTHER FRANCES
MARRIED BUSINESSMAN PETER SHAND KYDD BUT FAILED
TO GET CUSTODY OF HER CHILDREN. DIANA HAD A FIERY
RELATIONSHIP WITH HER MOTHER AND THE PAIR WOULD
FALL OUT FOR MONTHS AT A TIME. RECENTLY SHE DIDN'T
SPEAK TO HER MOTHER, WHO IS DEEPLY RELIGIOUS AND
LIVES ALONE IN SCOTLAND, BECAUSE SHE GAVE AN
INTERVIEW TO A MAGAZINE WITHOUT CONSULTING HER.

DIANA WAS BROUGHT UP BY HER FATHER, EARL
SPENCER, WHO MARRIED BARBARA CARTLAND'S
DAUGHTER RAINE IN 1976. RAINE NURSED HIM BACK
TO HEALTH AFTER A STROKE IN 1978 AND IT WAS THE
PROUDEST MOMENT OF HIS LIFE WHEN HE GAVE DI
AWAY IN ST PAUL'S CATHEDRAL IN 1981. DI ALWAYS
GOT ON WELL WITH HER DAD WHO DIED IN 1992.

DIANA'S TWO SISTERS, SARAH AND JANE WERE OLDER BY SIX AND FOUR YEARS RESPECTIVELY. SARAH WENT OUT WITH PRINCE CHARLES FIRST AND INTRODUCED HER SISTER TO HIM WHEN DIANA WAS JUST 16. SARAH, WHO SUFFERED FROM ANOREXIA, MARRIED FARMER NEIL MCCORQUODALE IN 1980. JANE MARRIED ROBERT FELLOWES WHO BECAME THE QUEEN'S SECRETARY AND WAS LATER KNIGHTED. HER RELATIONSHIP WITH HER SISTERS WAS PUT UNDER IMMENSE STRAIN WHEN HER MARRIAGE TO CHARLES FINALLY BROKE UP.

DIANA'S YOUNGER BROTHER CHARLES, NOW EARL SPENCER,
IN HIS MOVING TRIBUTE TO HIS SISTER, REFERRED TO HER
AS 'THE UNIQUE, THE COMPLEX, THE EXTRAORDINARY AND
IRREPLACEABLE DIANA, WHOSE BEAUTY, BOTH INTERNAL AND
EXTERNAL WILL NEVER BE EXTINGUISHED FROM OUR MINDS.'

DIANA GREW UP READING ROMANTIC NOVELS
BY BARBARA CARTLAND WHO, AS RAINE'S MOTHER,
AMAZINGLY BECAME THE PRINCESS'S STEP-GRAND-
MOTHER. THE PAIR ALWAYS GOT ON WELL.

THE PRINCESS WAS INSPIRED BY EX-CRICKET STAR
IMRAN KHAN AND HIS WIFE JEMIMA GOLDSMITH,
WHO SPARKED OFF HER INTEREST IN ALL THINGS
EASTERN. SHE VISITED IMRAN'S CANCER HOSPITAL
IN LAHORE AND WAS DEVASTATED WHEN IT WAS
LATER BOMBED BY POLITICAL TERRORISTS.

LUCIA FLECHA DE LIMA WAS ONCE DESCRIBED AS DIANA'S
SECOND MOTHER. SHE WAS AMONG THE TIGHT-KNIT
LONDON CIRCLE OF FRIENDS THAT THE PRINCESS RELIED ON
AS HER MARRIAGE BROKE UP. LUCIA, WIFE OF THE FORMER
BRAZILIAN AMBASSADOR TO LONDON, WAS A SHOULDER TO
CRY ON AND WHEN SHE MOVED ACROSS THE ATLANTIC, THE
TWO MAINTAINED A CLOSE FRIENDSHIP. DIANA HAD TWICE
VISITED MARTHA'S VINEYARD TO STAY WITH LUCIA AND
THERE WERE RUMOURS THAT DIANA WAS PLANNING A VISIT
TO INTRODUCE DODI TO HER AT THE TIME OF HER DEATH

CATHERINE WALKER WAS ONE OF THE PRINCESS'S FAVOURITE
DESIGNERS AND THE ONE CREDITED WITH DEVELOPING
DIANA'S ELEGANT SIGNATURE STYLE. OVER FIFTY OF HER
DRESSES WERE AMONG THE EIGHTY THAT DIANA AUCTIONED.
AND CATHERINE, WHO WAS DIAGNOSED WITH BREAST CANCER
TWO YEARS AGO, SAID SHE WAS DEEPLY MOVED WHEN THE
PRINCESS ANNOUNCED SOME OF THE MONEY FROM THE SALE
WOULD GO TOWARDS BREAST CANCER RESEARCH. 'I HAVE
RECEIVED UNFAILING SUPPORT FROM THE PRINCESS SINCE I
WAS DIAGNOSED WITH THE DISEASE,' SHE SAID IN A RARE
INTERVIEW BEFORE HER FAVOURITE CLIENT'S DEATH

EVEN IN HER LONELIEST MOMENTS DIANA NEVER WANTED
TO GET DIVORCED. 'WHAT ABOUT THE CHILDREN. OUR BOYS.
THAT'S WHAT MATTERS, ISN'T IT?' SHE TOLD BBC JOURNALIST
MARTIN BASHIR WHEN HE BROUGHT UP THE SUBJECT OF
DIVORCE DURING THEIR INTERVIEW. DIANA WAS PREPARED
TO SACRIFICE HER OWN HAPPINESS FOR THE SAKE OF HER
BELOVED SONS. SHE WAS DETERMINED THEY WOULD NOT
SUFFER LIKE SHE HAD FROM A BITTER DIVORCE. SADLY,
HISTORY REPEATED ITSELF. ONE OF HER OTHER BIGGEST
REGRETS, WAS THAT SHE HAD NEVER BEEN ABLE TO GIVE
THEM A BABY SISTER – SHE SAID PUBLICLY HOW MUCH
SHE LONGED FOR A DAUGHTER.

Diana

AS SHE SAW HERSELF

'At the age of 19, you always think you're prepared for everything, and you think you have the knowledge of what's coming ahead. But although I was daunted at the prospect at the time, I felt I had the support of my husband-to-be.'

Diana, Princess of Wales

This quote and all of the following come from Diana's 1995 interview on *Panorama* with Martin Bashir.

'I think like any marriage – especially when
you've had divorced parents like myself – you'd
want to try even harder to make it work, and
you don't want to fall back into a pattern that
you've seen happen in your own family.'

'I desperately wanted it to work; I desperately
loved my husband, and I wanted to share
everything together. I thought that we
were a very good team.'

'The most daunting aspect was the media attention, because my
husband and I... We were told when we got engaged the media
would go quietly, and it didn't. And then when we were
married, they said it would go quietly, and it didn't. And then
it started to focus very much on me and I seemed to be on
the front of a newspaper every single day, which is an
isolating experience, and the higher the media
put you, the bigger the drop.'

'It took a long time to understand why people were so
interested in me, but I assumed it was because my
husband had done a lot of wonderful work leading up
to our marriage and our relationship.'

'I was very daunted because, as far as I was concerned, I was a fat, chubby 20-year-old and I couldn't understand the level of interest.'

'The pressure on us both as a couple with the media was
phenomenal and misunderstood by a great many people.'

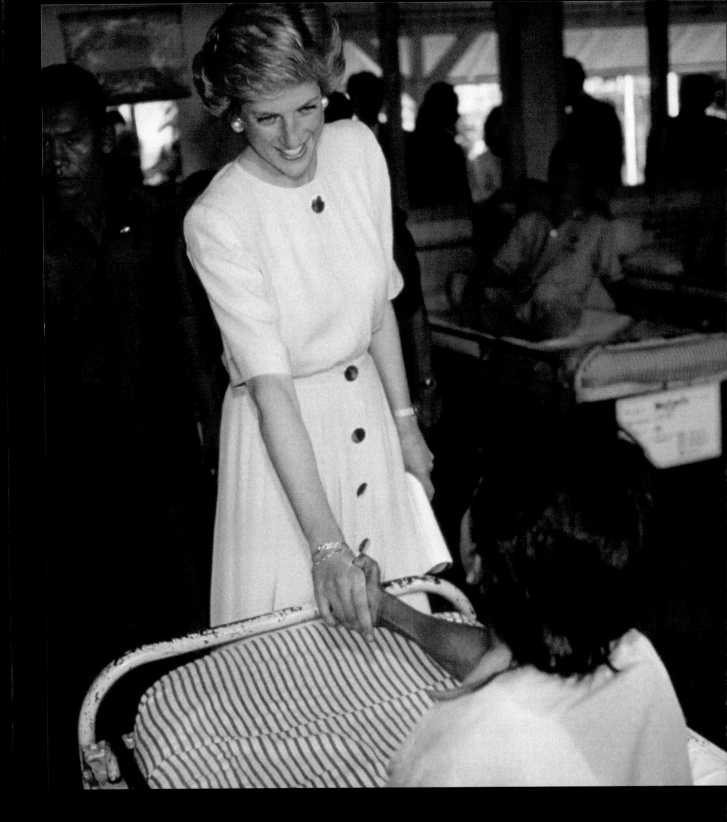

'I found myself being more and more involved with people who were rejected by society – with, I'd say, drug addicts, alcoholics, battered this, battered that – and I found an affinity there.'

'I respected very much the honesty I found on that level with people I met, because in hospices, for instance, when people are dying they're much more open and more vulnerable, and much more real than other people. And I appreciated that.'

'No one sat me down with a piece of paper and said: "This is what is expected of you". But I'm lucky enough in the fact that I have found my role, and I'm very conscious of it. I love being with people.'

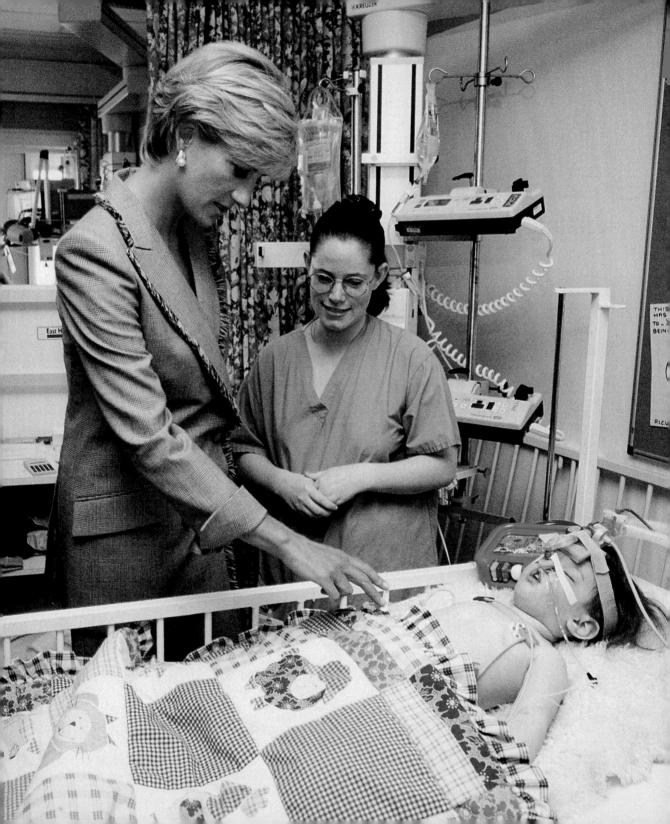

'I felt the whole country was in labour with me. But I had actually known William was going to be a boy, because the scan had shown it, so it caused no surprise.'

'Everybody was thrilled to bits. It had been quite a difficult pregnancy – I hadn't been very well throughout it – so by the time William arrived, it was a great relief, because it was all peaceful again and I was well for a time.'

'Then I was unwell with post-natal depression, which no one ever discusses – post-natal depression, you have to read about it afterwards, and that in itself was a bit of a difficult time. You'd wake up in the morning feeling you didn't want to get out of bed – you felt misunderstood and just very, very low in yourself.'

'I came from a family where there were four of us, so we had enormous fun there. And then William and Harry arrived – fortunately two boys, it would have been a little tricky if it had been two girls – but that in itself brings the responsibilities of bringing them up – William's future being as it is, and Harry like a form of a back-up in that aspect.'

'My husband and I had to keep everything together because we didn't want to disappoint the public, and yet obviously there was a lot of anxiety going on within our four walls.'

'I had bulimia for a number of years. And that's like a secret
disease. You inflict it upon yourself because your self-esteem is
at a low ebb and you don't think you're worthy or valuable.
You fill your stomach up four or five times a day – some do
it more – and it gives you a feeling of comfort.'

'It was a symptom of what was going on in my marriage.
I was crying out for help but giving the wrong signals, and
people were using my bulimia as a coat on a hanger – they
decided that was the problem: Diana was unstable.'

'It was difficult to share that load, because I was the one
who was always pitched out front, whether it was my clothes,
what I said, what my hair was doing, everything – which was a
pretty dull subject, actually, and it's been exhausted over the
years – when actually what we wanted to have, what we wanted
supported, was our work as a team.'

'I was portrayed in the media at that time, if I remember
rightly, as someone... because I hadn't passed any O-levels and
taken any A-levels, I was stupid. And I made the grave mistake
once of saying to a child that I was as thick as a plank in order
to ease the child's nervousness, which it did. But that headline
went all around the world and I rather regret saying it.'

'Well, there were three of us in this marriage,
so it was a bit crowded.'

'My husband and I struggled along. We did our engagements
together. And in our private life, it was obviously turbulent.'

'My husband and I, we discussed it very calmly. We could see
what the public were requiring. They wanted clarity of a
situation that was obviously becoming intolerable.'

'I still, to this day, find the interest [in me] daunting
and phenomenal, because I actually don't like
being the centre of attention.'

'He [James Hewitt] was a great friend of mine at a very difficult, yet another difficult time, and he was always there to support me. I was absolutely devastated when this book appeared, because I trusted him and because, again, I worried about the effect on my children.'

'And yes, there was factual evidence in the book, but a lot of it didn't equate to what happened.'

'He'd rung me up 10 days before it arrived in the bookshops to tell me there was nothing to worry about and I believed him, stupidly.'

'When it did arrive, the first thing I did was rush down to talk to my children. And William produced a box of chocolates and said, "Mummy I think you've been hurt. These are to make you smile again".'

'Yes, I adored him. Yes, I was in love with him. But I was very let down.'

'I'd like to be an ambassador for this country.'

'I'm not a political animal, but I think the biggest disease this
world suffers from in this day and age is the disease of people
feeling unloved, and I know that I can give love for a minute,
for half an hour, for a day, for a month, but I can give –
I'm very happy to do that, and I want to do that.'

'I think the British people need someone in public life to give
affection, to make them feel important, to support them...'

'I mean, once or twice, I've heard people say to me that, you know, "Diana's out to destroy the monarchy", which has bewildered me, because why would i want to destroy something that is my children's future.'

Diana

HER UNIQUE STYLE

IN A VERSACE DESIGN, DIANA CERTAINLY TURNED HE
WHEN SHE ARRIVED FOR A GALA DINNER IN CHICAG

MANY OF THE DRESSES DIANA WORE FOR STATE OCCASIONS
WERE INCLUDED IN HER NEW YORK CHARITY AUCTION

DIANA DONATED 79 DIFFERENT BALLGOWNS AND
COCKTAIL DRESSES FOR THE GRAND SALE

IN RECENT YEARS, SHE FAVOURED CLEAN, CLASSIC
LINES RATHER THAN THE GLITZ OF THE EIGHTIES

OUT WENT THE FRILLS AND FLOUNCES, IN FAVOUR OF
THE CHIC STRAPLESS GOWNS BY CATHERINE WALKER

AS ONE OF THE MOST PHOTOGRAPHED WOMEN IN THE
WORLD, DIANA KNEW HOW TO MAKE AN ENTRANCE

FOR ALL HER EVENING GOWNS, MATCHING
ACCESSORIES ALWAYS COMPLETED DIANA'S LOOK

AT THE AUCTION, DIANA SAID GOODBYE TO MANY
FAVOURITE DRESSES AND PUT HER PAST BEHIND HER

...the massively successful New York charity auction of some of her best remembered cocktail dresses and ballgowns earlier this year proved, Diana Princess of Wales, was renowned throughout the world as a fashion icon. Her style and elegance were copied and revered everywhere she went, bringing sophistication and glamour to the British royal family and making her the most photographed woman in the world.

The sale of the collection of outfits provided a telling glimpse of Diana's life as a royal and her transition from ingenue to confident single woman. All were seen by the Princess as part of her past.

After 16 years in the public spotlight, the world looked on as the young Diana Spencer matured from the mousy-haired, rather awkward-looking 19-year-old, kindergarten teacher – most memorably photographed in that flimsy see-through floral skirt – into the stylish, sophisticated Princess, totally at ease with her polished appearance.

After stepping from relative obscurity to marrying into one of the world's most well known families, the Princess quickly learned that appearance was everything. In those early, heady days of her marriage to Prince Charles, she made a point of video-taping every one of her many television appearances and studying, with a critical eye, every single detail of her appearance from her outfit, to her hair, her clothes and her make-up. She rose to every daunting state occasion, both home and abroad, by making

sure she looked the part and choosing her outfits carefully – during an early royal tour with Prince Charles to Japan in 1986, she even chose to wear a white and red spotted silk dress reflecting the design of the Japanese flag.

As her role was to change over the years, so did her style. During the early Eighties her favourite outfits had included plenty of flamboyant detail, worn with hats, tiaras and lots of jewellery. The Princess epitomised romance, and then, influenced by the glitz of the mid-Eighties, she traded the bows for sequins during her 'Dynasty Di' phase. This was followed by her high-glam look: when single-sleeved gowns and column dresses with boleros became her trademark.

As her clothes changed over the years, so did her hair. From the simple, straight bob of those early days in front of the camera, she progressed to the big, blonde hair to match the glamorous gowns and sparkling tiaras.

Then as the rift in her marriage became more and more apparent, there was also a noticeable change in her style. She adopted a more minimalist look with very few hats, and very little jewellery except for her favourite pearls and usually only a matching bag with gold clasp or chain to round off her outfit. Her hair was cut shorter and sleeker and everything in her wardrobe became very low-key, choosing such London-based designers as Catherine Walker and Bruce Oldfield.

With her divorce from Prince Charles finalised just

over a year ago, not only did the Princess forge herself new role, she also evolved new look. As she concentrat more and more on the type 'hands-on' work' she loved t most – she remained one Britain's finest ambassado abroad and threw hers wholeheartedly into her char work, remaining as acti patron of six charities includ the national Aids Trust a Great Ormond Street Childre Hospital – her wardro adapted accordingly to the l formal surroundings.

When she visited Ango this year, as part of involvement in the anti la mine campaign, she wor simple cotton blouse a trousers, wanting the worl focus on the campaign and on what she was wearing.

When Prince Willi suggested auctioning some her many dresses for char the Princess leapt at the ic Here was the chance to some of those much-p tographed and much-admi designer outfits to good and raise money for cau close to her heart – The Ro Marsden Hospital Cancer Fu and the Aids Crisis Trust. resulting auction held Christie's, New York, on J 25 1997, raised a phenom £1,960,150.

It was the perfect way Diana to finally put her behind her. The independ Princess, free of the c straints of Palace life, finally come to a clea understanding of who she which was reflected in uncluttered, unfussy supremely elegant clothes chose to wear.

Diana

HER RELATIONSHIPS

AS HER MARRIAGE BEGAN TO FAIL, DIANA'S FRIENDSHIP
WITH YOUNG CAVALRY OFFICER, JAMES HEWITT,
BLOSSOMED INTO AN AFFAIR. IN 1994 HE BETRAYED
HER BY 'TELLING ALL' IN A BOOK. OLIVER HOARE (RIGHT)
WAS THE SUBJECT OF ALLEGED LATE NIGHT CALLS BY
DIANA – BUT SHE STRONGLY DENIED MAKING THEM.

IN AUGUST 1995 DIANA WAS LINKED WITH MARRIED
ENGLAND RUGBY CAPTAIN, WILL CARLING. BOTH DENIED
AN AFFAIR. TWO MONTHS LATER, THE CARLINGS SPLIT UP.
IN JUNE OF THIS YEAR, DIANA WENT DANCING WITH
DIVORCED ELECTRONICS TYCOON GULU LALVANI, (RIGHT)
23 YEARS HER SENIOR. HE SAID: 'WE'RE JUST FRIENDS.'

DURING 1997 DIANA WAS ALSO LINKED TO LONDON
DOCTOR HASNAT KHAN, BUT A FEW WEEKS AFTER SHE
WAS RUMOURED TO BE SEEKING A MARRIAGE TO HIM,
SHE WAS PICTURED ON HOLIDAY WITH DODI FAYED,
SON OF HARRODS OWNER MOHAMED. IT WAS TO BE
HER LAST, AND PERHAPS HAPPIEST, LOVE AFFAIR

The
New
Diana

THE STRAIN OF BEING THE WORLD'S MOST WATCHED
AND PHOTOGRAPHED WOMAN TOOK ITS TOLL AND,
IN DECEMBER 1993, A TEARFUL DIANA (ABOVE)
ANNOUNCED THAT SHE WAS CUTTING BACK ON HER
PUBLIC DUTIES. BUT PICTURED AT A BENEFIT FOR
ST JOHN'S HOSPICE IN NORTH LONDON IN 1997 (RIGHT)
DIANA'S SMILE REVEALED THAT SHE HAD COME TO
TERMS WITH SOME OF THE INSECURITY THAT
DOGGED HER THROUGH THE EARLY YEARS

IN NOVEMBER 1995, THE PRINCESS GAVE
HER MOST SENSATIONAL INTERVIEW EVER TO
PANORAMA'S MARTIN BASHIR. SHE SPOKE FRANKLY
ABOUT HER UNHAPPY RELATIONSHIP WITH THE ROYAL
FAMILY, HER EATING DISORDERS AND HER HUSBAND'S
ADULTERY. DIANA REVEALED SHE NEVER BELIEVED SHE
WOULD BECOME QUEEN OF ENGLAND AND WANTED TO
BE SEEN INSTEAD AS 'A QUEEN OF PEOPLE'S HEARTS'.
NINE MONTHS AFTER GIVING THE INTERVIEW,
THE DIVORCE WAS FINALISED AND DIANA WAS A
SINGLE WOMAN AGAIN. DURING THESE TROUBLED
TIMES, SHE MAINTAINED HER FITNESS REGIME AND
WAS FREQUENTLY PHOTOGRAPHED AS SHE
ARRIVED AND LEFT THE GYM

DESPITE CUTTING DOWN ON HER OFFICIAL DUTIES,
DIANA CONTINUED HER CHARITABLE WORKS WHICH
INCLUDED HELPING RAISE FUNDS FOR IMRAN KHAN'S
CANCER HOSPITAL IN LAHORE, PAKISTAN, AND
ATTENDING A GALA HELD BY THE AMERICAN RED CROSS
IN AID OF LAND MINE VICTIMS AROUND THE WORLD

DIANA'S HUMANITARIAN WORK WILL REMAIN ONE OF
HER MOST ENDURING LEGACIES. TONY BLAIR HAD AN
AMBASSADORIAL ROLE IN MIND FOR HER. SHE HIT THE HEAD-
LINES IN JANUARY THIS YEAR WHEN SHE VISITED LAND MINE
VICTIMS IN ANGOLA. SADLY, MOTHER TERESA, WHOM DIANA
VISITED IN NEW YORK IN JUNE, PASSED AWAY ON THE EVE OF
THE FUNERAL. SHE WAS 'HEARTBROKEN' BY DIANA'S DEATH
AND PAID TRIBUTE TO HER, SAYING: 'SHE HELPED ME TO
HELP THE POOR, AND THAT'S THE MOST BEAUTIFUL THING.'

Diana

THE TRIBUTES

CANDLE IN THE WIND – ELTON JOHN

GOODBYE ENGLAND'S ROSE;
MAY YOU EVER GROW IN OUR HEARTS.
YOU WERE THE GRACE THAT PLACED ITSELF
WHERE LIVES WERE TORN APART.
YOU CALLED OUT TO OUR COUNTRY,
AND YOU WHISPERED TO THOSE IN PAIN.
NOW YOU BELONG TO HEAVEN,
AND THE STARS SPELL OUT YOUR NAME.

AND IT SEEMS TO ME YOU LIVED YOUR LIFE
LIKE A CANDLE IN THE WIND:
NEVER FADING WITH THE SUNSET
WHEN THE RAIN SET IN.
AND YOUR FOOTSTEPS WILL
ALWAYS FALL HERE,
ALONG ENGLAND'S GREENEST HILLS;
YOUR CANDLE'S BURNED OUT
LONG BEFORE
YOUR LEGEND EVER WILL.

LOVELINESS WE'VE LOST;
THESE EMPTY DAYS WITHOUT YOUR SMILE.
THIS TORCH WE'LL ALWAYS CARRY
FOR OUR NATION'S GOLDEN CHILD.
AND EVEN THOUGH WE TRY,
THE TRUTH BRINGS US TO TEARS;
ALL OUR WORDS CANNOT EXPRESS
THE JOY YOU BROUGHT US
THROUGH THE YEARS.

GOODBYE ENGLAND'S ROSE,
FROM A COUNTRY LOST
WITHOUT YOUR SOUL,
WHO'LL MISS THE WINGS OF
YOUR COMPASSION
MORE THAN YOU'LL EVER KNOW.

NEVER HAD SUCH A BROAD SPECTRUM OF MOURNERS
COLLECTED UNDER THE STONE VAULTS OF WESTMINSTER
ABBEY. THE MOURNING FAMILY WERE JOINED IN GRIEF
BY SUPERSTARS GEORGE MICHAEL, STING AND ELTON
JOHN. HOLLYWOOD WAS REPRESENTED BY TOM HANKS,
NICOLE KIDMAN, TOM CRUISE AND STEVEN SPIELBERG.
AND AMONGST THE TRIBUTES PAID TO THE PRINCESS
OF WALES, ONE WAS UNIQUE: ELTON JOHN SANG A
SPECIALLY REWRITTEN *CANDLE IN THE WIND* FOR HER.

DIANA, PRINCESS OF WALES, MADE A FINAL JOURNEY
HOME ON SATURDAY SEPTEMBER 6. AS SPECIFIED IN
HER WILL, THE FORMER LADY DIANA SPENCER WAS
LAID TO REST AT HER FAMILY'S ALTHORP ESTATE IN
NORTHAMPTONSHIRE. AFTER THE SERVICE IN LONDON,
HER BODY WAS CARRIED BY HEARSE THROUGH NORTH
LONDON SUBURBS AND ALONG THE M1 – CROWDS STILL
LINING THE ROUTE AND THROWING FLOWERS IN ITS
PATH. IN THE GROUNDS OF THE HOUSE WHERE SHE
GREW UP, HER SONS, PRINCE CHARLES, HER SISTERS, HER
MOTHER AND HER BROTHER, THE EARL SPENCER, MADE
THEIR FINAL FAREWELLS TO THEIR BELOVED DIANA.

A NARROW CINDER PATH LEADS DOWN TO THE
CALM GLASS-LIKE OVAL LAKE IN THE GARDENS OF THE
ALTHORP ESTATE. IT'S A PLACE WHERE DIANA SPENCER
OFTEN USED TO WALK AND THINK. IT'S WHERE THE
PRINCESS OF WALES FOUND A QUIET HAVEN DURING
THE FESTIVITIES OF HER BROTHER'S WEDDING. AND IT
IS ON THE ISLAND IN THE CENTRE OF THE LAKE THAT
DIANA, PRINCESS OF WALES, HAS FOUND PEACE AT LAST